Brunch

Discover the Joys of Brunch with Easy Brunch Recipes

By
BookSumo Press

Published by
http://www.booksumo.com

LEGAL NOTES

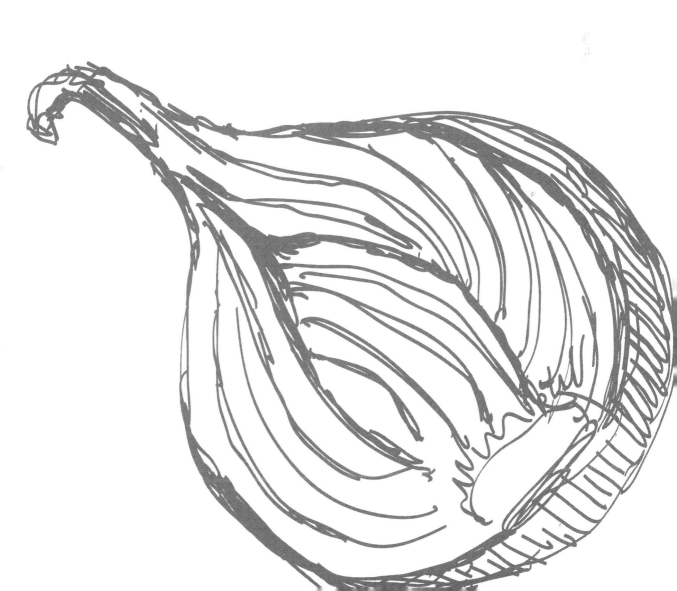

Table of Contents

Athenian
Pasta Salad
(Greek)

Prep Time: 15 mins
Total Time: 2 hrs 25 mins

Servings per Recipe: 4
Calories	746 kcal
Carbohydrates	40.4 g
Cholesterol	70 mg
Fat	56.1 g
Protein	22.1 g
Sodium	1279 mg

Ingredients

1/2 cup olive oil
1/2 cup red wine vinegar
1 1/2 tsps garlic powder
1 1/2 tsps dried basil
1 1/2 tsps dried oregano
3/4 tsp ground black pepper
3/4 tsp white sugar
2 1/2 cups cooked elbow macaroni
3 cups fresh sliced mushrooms

15 cherry tomatoes, halved
1 cup sliced red bell peppers
3/4 cup crumbled feta cheese
1/2 cup chopped green onions
1 (4 ounce) can whole black olives
3/4 cup sliced pepperoni sausage, cut into strips

Directions

1. Combine all the ingredients mentioned above in a bowl very thoroughly before covering it up and refrigerating it for at least 2 hours.

2. Serve.

FETA-FARFALLE
Pasta Salad

Prep Time: 10 mins
Total Time: 2 hrs 25 mins

Servings per Recipe: 6

Calories	334 kcal
Carbohydrates	41.8 g
Cholesterol	6 mg
Fat	16.6 g
Protein	8.6 g
Sodium	1167 mg

Ingredients

1 (12 ounce) package farfalle pasta
10 ounces baby spinach, rinsed and torn into bite-size piece
2 ounces crumbled feta cheese with basil and tomato
1 red onion, chopped
1 (15 ounce) can black olives, drained and chopped

1 cup Italian-style salad dressing
4 cloves garlic, minced
1 lemon, juiced
1/2 tsp garlic salt
1/2 tsp ground black pepper

Directions

1. Cook pasta in salty boiling water for about 10 minutes until tender before draining it.
2. Coat a mixture of pasta, olives, spinach, red onion and cheese with a mixture of salad dressing, pepper, lemon juice, salt and garlic very thoroughly before refrigerating it for at least two hours.
3. Serve.

Caesar
Parmesan Pasta Salad

🥣 Prep Time: 15 mins
🕐 Total Time: 30 mins

Servings per Recipe: 12
Calories	291 kcal
Carbohydrates	32.6 g
Cholesterol	6 mg
Fat	14.6 g
Protein	8.5 g
Sodium	728 mg

Ingredients

1 (16 ounce) package rotini pasta
1 cup Italian-style salad dressing
1 cup creamy Caesar salad dressing
1 cup grated Parmesan cheese

1 red bell pepper, diced
1 green bell pepper, chopped
1 red onion, diced

Directions

1. Cook pasta in salty boiling water for about 10 minutes until tender before draining it.

2. Mix pasta, red bell pepper, Italian salad dressing, Caesar dressing, Parmesan cheese, green bell pepper and red onion very thoroughly before refrigerating for a few hours.

3. Serve.

HEALTHY
Pasta Salad

Prep Time: 15 mins
Total Time: 30 mins

Servings per Recipe: 12
Calories	289 kcal
Carbohydrates	34.6 g
Cholesterol	8 mg
Fat	13.9 g
Protein	10 g
Sodium	764 mg

Ingredients

1 (16 ounce) package uncooked rotini pasta
1 (16 ounce) bottle Italian salad dressing
2 cucumbers, chopped
6 tomatoes, chopped

1 bunch green onions, chopped
4 ounces grated Parmesan cheese
1 tbsp Italian seasoning

Directions

1. Cook pasta in salty boiling water for about 10 minutes until tender before draining it.
2. Coat a mixture of pasta, green onions, cucumbers and tomatoes with a mixture of parmesan cheese and Italian seasoning very thoroughly before refrigerating it covered for a few hours.
3. Serve.

Vegetable
Pasta Salad

🥣 Prep Time: 10 mins

🕐 Total Time: 25 mins

Servings per Recipe: 8

Calories	181 kcal
Carbohydrates	38.1 g
Cholesterol	0 mg
Fat	0.7 g
Protein	5.4 g
Sodium	238 mg

Ingredients

10 ounces fusilli pasta
1 onion, chopped
1 green bell pepper, chopped
2 tomatoes, chopped

1 cup chopped mushrooms
3/4 cup fat free Italian-style dressing

Directions

1. Cook pasta in salty boiling water for about 10 minutes until tender before draining it.

2. Mix pasta, mushrooms, onions, tomatoes and bell pepper very thoroughly before refrigerating for at least one hour.

3. Serve.

GRILLED
Pasta Salad

Prep Time: 15 mins
Total Time: 45 mins

Servings per Recipe: 4

Calories	504 kcal
Carbohydrates	48 g
Cholesterol	103 mg
Fat	13.2 g
Protein	46.5 g
Sodium	650 mg

Ingredients

4 skinless, boneless chicken breast halves
steak seasoning to taste
8 ounces rotini pasta
8 ounces mozzarella cheese, cubed

1 red onion, chopped
1 head romaine lettuce, chopped
6 cherry tomatoes, chopped

Directions

1. At first you need to set grill at medium heat and put some oil before starting anything else.
2. Coat chicken breast with steak seasoning before cooking it on the preheated grill for 8 minutes each side.
3. Cook pasta in salty boiling water for about 10 minutes until tender before draining it.
4. Add mixture of tomatoes, cheese, onion and lettuce into the bowl containing pasta and chicken.
5. Mix it thoroughly before serving.

Best
Breakfast Muffins

Prep Time: 15 mins
Total Time: 35 mins

Servings per Recipe: 18
Calories	194 kcal
Fat	4.2 g
Carbohydrates	37.3g
Protein	3.1 g
Cholesterol	10 mg
Sodium	175 mg

Ingredients

1 1/2 C. all-purpose flour
1/2 C. whole wheat flour
1 1/4 C. white sugar
1 tbsp ground cinnamon
2 tsp baking powder
1/2 tsp baking soda
1/2 tsp salt
2 C. grated carrots
1 apple - peeled, cored, and chopped

1 C. raisins
1 egg
2 egg whites
1/2 C. apple butter
1/4 C. vegetable oil
1 tbsp vanilla extract
2 tbsp chopped walnuts
2 tbsp toasted wheat germ

Directions

1. Set your oven to 375 degrees F before doing anything else and lightly, grease 18 cups of the muffin pans.
2. In a bowl, add the eggs, egg whites, apple butter, oil and vanilla and beat till well combined.
3. In another large bowl, mix together the flours, sugar, cinnamon, baking powder, baking soda and salt.
4. Add the carrots, apples and raisins and stir to combine.
5. Add the egg mixture and mix till just moistened.
6. Transfer the mixture into the prepared muffin cups about 3/4 full.
7. In a small bowl, mix together the walnuts and wheat germ and sprinkle over the top of muffins.
8. Cook in the oven for about 15-20 minutes or till a toothpick inserted in the center comes out clean.

AUTUMNAL
Muffins

Prep Time: 15 mins
Total Time: 1 hr

Servings per Recipe: 18

Calories	249 kcal
Fat	8 g
Carbohydrates	42.6g
Protein	2.8 g
Cholesterol	23 mg
Sodium	182 mg

Ingredients

2 1/2 C. all-purpose flour
2 C. white sugar
1 tbsp pumpkin pie spice
1 tsp baking soda
1/2 tsp salt
2 eggs, lightly beaten
1 C. canned pumpkin puree
1/2 C. vegetable oil

2 C. peeled, cored and chopped apple
2 tbsp all-purpose flour
1/4 C. white sugar
1/2 tsp ground cinnamon
4 tsp butter

Directions

1. Set your oven to 375 degrees F before doing anything else and lightly, grease 18 cups of the muffin pans.
2. In a large bowl, sift together 2 1/2 C. of the all-purpose flour, 2 C. of the sugar, pumpkin pie spice, baking soda and salt.
3. In another bowl, add the eggs, pumpkin and oil and beat till well combined.
4. Add the pumpkin mixture into the flour mixture and mix till just moistened.
5. Fold in the apples.
6. Transfer the mixture into the prepared muffin cups evenly.
7. In a small bowl, mix together 2 tbsp of the flour, 1/4 C. of the sugar and 1/2 tsp of the cinnamon.
8. With a pastry cutter, cut the butter and mix till a coarse crumb forms.
9. Sprinkle the crumb mixture over the top of muffins.
10. Cook in the oven for about 35-40 minutes or till a toothpick inserted in the center comes out clean.

Flax Raisin
and Vanilla Muffins

🥣 Prep Time: 15 mins
🕐 Total Time: 35 mins

Servings per Recipe: 15
Calories	272 kcal
Fat	11 g
Carbohydrates	40.9 g
Protein	6.7 g
Cholesterol	25 mg
Sodium	449 mg

Ingredients

1 1/2 C. all-purpose flour
3/4 C. ground flax seed
3/4 C. oat bran
1 C. brown sugar
2 tsp baking soda
1 tsp baking powder
1 tsp salt
2 tsp ground cinnamon
3/4 C. skim milk

2 eggs, beaten
1 tsp vanilla extract
2 tbsp vegetable oil
2 C. shredded carrots
2 apples, peeled, shredded
1/2 C. raisins
1 C. chopped mixed nuts

Directions

1. Set your oven to 350 degrees F before doing anything else and grease 15 cups of the muffin pans.
2. In a large bowl, mix together the flour, flax seed, oat bran, brown sugar, baking soda, baking powder, salt and cinnamon.
3. Add the milk, eggs, vanilla and oil and mix till just moistened.
4. Fold in the carrots, apples, raisins and nuts.
5. Transfer the mixture into the prepared muffin cups about 2/3 full.
6. Cook in the oven for about 15-20 minutes or till a toothpick inserted in the center comes out clean.

DUTCH STYLE
Muffins

Prep Time: 15 mins
Total Time: 40 mins

Servings per Recipe: 12	
Calories	312 kcal
Fat	10.5 g
Carbohydrates	51.1g
Protein	4.2 g
Cholesterol	42 mg
Sodium	306 mg

Ingredients

2 1/4 C. all-purpose flour
1 tsp baking soda
1/2 tsp salt
1 egg
1 C. buttermilk
1/2 C. butter, melted
1 tsp vanilla extract
1 1/2 C. packed brown sugar

2 C. diced apples
1/2 C. packed brown sugar
1/3 C. all-purpose flour
1 tsp ground cinnamon
2 tbsp butter, melted

Directions

1. Set your oven to 375 degrees F before doing anything else and lightly, grease 12 cups of a muffin pan.
2. In a large bowl, mix together 2 1/4 C. of the flour, baking soda and salt.
3. In another smaller bowl, add the egg, buttermilk, 1/2 C. of the melted butter, vanilla and 1 1/2 C. of the brown sugar and beat till sugar dissolves.
4. Add the egg mixture and apples into the flour mixture and mix till just combined.
5. Transfer the mixture into the prepared muffin cups, filling to the top.
6. In a small bowl, mix together 1/2 C. of the brown sugar, 1/3 C. of the flour and cinnamon.
7. Drizzle in 2 tbsp of the melted butter while mixing with a fork till well combined.
8. Sprinkle the brown sugar mixture over the muffin tops.
9. Cook in the oven for about 25 minutes or till a toothpick inserted in the center comes out clean.

Buttermilk Blueberry Muffins

🥣 Prep Time: 15 mins
🕐 Total Time: 30 mins

Servings per Recipe: 12
Calories	196 kcal
Fat	5.8 g
Carbohydrates	33.4g
Protein	5.1 g
Cholesterol	16 mg
Sodium	223 mg

Ingredients

3/4 C. all-purpose flour
3/4 C. whole wheat flour
3/4 C. white sugar
1/4 C. oat bran
1/4 C. quick cooking oats
1/4 C. wheat germ
1 tsp baking powder
1 tsp baking soda
1/4 tsp salt

1 C. blueberries
1/2 C. chopped walnuts
1 banana, mashed
1 C. buttermilk
1 egg
1 tbsp vegetable oil
1 tsp vanilla extract

Directions

1. Set your oven to 350 degrees F before doing anything else and lightly, grease 12 cups of a muffin pan.
2. In a large bowl, mix together the flours, sugar, oat bran, quick-cooking oats, wheat germ, baking powder, baking soda and salt.
3. Gently, stir in the blueberries and walnuts.
4. In another bowl, add the mashed banana, buttermilk, egg, oil and vanilla and beat till well combined.
5. Add the egg mixture into the flour mixture and mix till just combined.
6. Transfer the mixture into the prepared muffin cups, filling to the top.
7. Cook in the oven for about 15-18 minutes or till a toothpick inserted in the center comes out clean.

CHOCO-VEGGIE
Muffins

Prep Time: 15 mins
Total Time: 50 mins

Servings per Recipe: 12
Calories   265 kcal
Fat   15.2 g
Carbohydrates   30.6g
Protein   3.5 g
Cholesterol   16 mg
Sodium   212 mg

Ingredients

1 1/2 C. all-purpose flour
3/4 C. white sugar
1 tsp baking soda
1 tsp ground cinnamon
1/2 tsp salt
1 egg, lightly beaten
1/2 C. vegetable oil
1/4 C. milk

1 tbsp lemon juice
1 tsp vanilla extract
1 C. shredded zucchini
1/2 C. miniature semisweet chocolate chips
1/2 C. chopped walnuts

Directions

1. Set your oven to 350 degrees F before doing anything else and lightly, grease 12 cups of a muffin pan.
2. In a large bowl, mix together the flour, sugar, baking soda, cinnamon and salt.
3. In another bowl, add the egg, oil, milk, lemon juice and vanilla extract and beat till well combined.
4. Add the egg mixture into the flour mixture and mix till just moistened.
5. Fold in the zucchini, chocolate chips and walnuts.
6. Transfer the mixture into the prepared muffin cups about 2/3 full.
7. Cook in the oven for about 20-25 minutes or till a toothpick inserted in the center comes out clean.

September's
Pumpkin Muffins

Prep Time: 15 mins
Total Time: 35 mins

Servings per Recipe: 12
Calories	263 kcal
Fat	13 g
Carbohydrates	35.9g
Protein	4.2 g
Cholesterol	31 mg
Sodium	224 mg

Ingredients

1/2 C. raisins
1 1/2 C. whole wheat flour
1/2 C. packed brown sugar
1 tsp pumpkin pie spice
3/4 tsp baking powder
1/2 tsp baking soda
1/2 tsp salt
2 eggs
3/4 C. canned pumpkin puree

1/2 C. vegetable oil
1/2 C. honey
1/2 C. chopped walnuts

Directions

1. Set your oven to 350 degrees F before doing anything else and grease 12 cups of a muffin pan.
2. In a bowl of hot water, soak the raisins for a few minutes.
3. In a large bowl, stir together the whole wheat flour, brown sugar, pumpkin pie spice, baking powder, baking soda and salt.
4. Make a well in the center of the flour mixture.
5. In the well, add the eggs, pumpkin, oil and honey and mix till just moistened.
6. Drain the raisins completely.
7. In the flour mixture, fold in the raisins and walnuts.
8. Transfer the mixture into the prepared muffin cups about 2/3 full.
9. Cook in the oven for about 18 minutes or till a toothpick inserted in the center comes out clean.
10. Remove from the oven and cool before turning out onto wire rack to cool completely.

EASTER
Brunch Pancakes

Prep Time: 15 mins
Total Time: 40 mins

Servings per Recipe: 8
Calories	360 kcal
Fat	19.5 g
Carbohydrates	31.2g
Protein	15.1 g
Cholesterol	89 mg
Sodium	792 mg

Ingredients

2 C. baking mix (such as Bisquick (R))
2 C. shredded Cheddar cheese, divided
1 C. milk
5 tbsp maple syrup
2 eggs

1 1/2 tbsp white sugar
12 slices cooked turkey bacon, crumbled

Directions

1. Set your oven to 350 degrees F before doing anything else and grease a 13x9-inch baking dish.

2. In a bowl, add the baking mix, 1 C. of the Cheddar cheese, milk, maple syrup, eggs and sugar and mix till well combined.

3. Transfer the mixture into the prepared baking dish.

4. Cook in the oven for about 20-25 minutes or till a toothpick inserted in the center comes out clean.

5. Remove from the oven and top the casserole with the bacon and remaining 1 C. of the Cheddar cheese evenly.

6. Cook in the oven for about 5 minutes.

Turkish Style
Pancakes

Prep Time: 15 mins
Total Time: 1 hr 20 mins

Servings per Recipe: 8

Calories	86 kcal
Fat	3.5 g
Carbohydrates	10g
Protein	3.5 g
Cholesterol	48 mg
Sodium	124 mg

Ingredients

2/3 C. water
2/3 C. milk
2 eggs
1 tbsp vegetable oil

1/3 tsp salt
3/4 C. all-purpose flour

Directions

1. In a bowl, add the water, milk, eggs, vegetable oil and salt and beat till well combined.
2. Slowly, add the flour into egg mixture and beat till well combined.
3. Keep the mixture aside for about 1 hour.
4. Stir the mixture again.
5. Heat a lightly greased griddle on medium-high heat.
6. Add the mixture by large spoonfuls into the griddle and cook for about 2-4 minutes per side.
7. Repeat with the remaining mixture.

3-INGREDIENT
Fruit Banana Pancakes

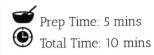

Prep Time: 5 mins
Total Time: 10 mins

Servings per Recipe: 2
Calories   93 kcal
Fat   2.7 g
Carbohydrates   14.9 g
Protein   3.8 g
Cholesterol   93 mg
Sodium   36 mg

Ingredients

1 banana, mashed
1 egg
1 tsp arrowroot powder

Directions

1. In a blender, add the banana, egg and arrowroot powder and pulse till well combined.
2. Heat a griddle on medium heat.
3. Place half of the mixture into the griddle and cook for about 2-3 minutes per side.
4. Repeat with the remaining mixture.

Healthy
Breakfast Pancakes

Prep Time: 10 mins
Total Time: 20 mins

Servings per Recipe: 4
Calories	304 kcal
Fat	2.7 g
Carbohydrates	64.6g
Protein	9.6 g
Cholesterol	0 mg
Sodium	734 mg

Ingredients

2 C. white whole wheat flour
2 tbsp baking powder
2 tbsp ground flax meal
17 fluid oz. orange juice

1 tsp orange extract

Directions

1. In a bowl, mix together the flour, baking powder and flax meal.
2. Add the orange juice and orange extract into flour mixture and mix till well-combined.
3. Heat a lightly greased griddle on medium-high heat.
4. Add the mixture by large spoonfuls into the griddle and cook for about 3-4 minutes.
5. Flip and cook for about 2-3 minutes.
6. Repeat with the remaining mixture.

APPLE
Cinnamon
Pancakes

Prep Time: 15 mins
Total Time: 30 mins

Servings per Recipe: 2

Calories	654 kcal
Fat	28.4 g
Carbohydrates	86g
Protein	16.6 g
Cholesterol	421 mg
Sodium	525 mg

Ingredients

3 tbsp butter
1 large apple, cored and sliced
1/2 C. white sugar, divided
2 tsp ground cinnamon
4 eggs
1/3 C. milk

1/3 C. all-purpose flour
1 tsp baking powder
1 tsp vanilla extract
1 pinch salt

Directions

1. Set your oven to 400 degrees F before doing anything else.
2. In an oven proof skillet, melt the butter on medium heat.
3. Add the apple slices, 1/4 C. of the sugar and cinnamon and cook, stirring for about 5 minutes.
4. Meanwhile in a large bowl, add the eggs, milk, flour, remaining 1/4 C. of the sugar, baking powder, vanilla extract and salt and beat till smooth.
5. Place the mixture over the apple slices evenly.
6. Cook in the oven for about 10 minutes.
7. Remove from the oven and run a spatula around the edges of the pancake to loosen.
8. Invert the skillet over a large plate and serve.

Peanut Butter Chocolate Pancakes

🥣 Prep Time: 15 mins
🕐 Total Time: 40 mins

Servings per Recipe: 4
Calories	484 kcal
Fat	23.4 g
Carbohydrates	58.2g
Protein	13.5 g
Cholesterol	77 mg
Sodium	737 mg

Ingredients

1 1/4 C. all-purpose flour
1 tbsp baking powder
1/2 tsp salt
2 tbsp brown sugar
1 1/2 C. milk
1 egg, beaten
3 tbsp butter, melted

1 tsp vanilla extract
1/4 C. peanut butter
1/4 C. chocolate chips
1 ripe banana, diced

Directions

1. In a bowl, mix together the flour, baking powder, salt and brown sugar.
2. In another bowl, add the egg and milk and beat till well combined.
3. Add the peanut butter and stir till smooth.
4. Add the milk mixture into the flour mixture and mix till just moistened.
5. Add the melted butter and vanilla extract and beat to combine.
6. Gently fold in the chocolate chips and diced banana.
7. Heat a large nonstick skillet on medium heat.
8. Add about 1/4 C. of the mixture into the skillet and cook for about 2 minutes.
9. Flip and cook for about 2-3 minutes.
10. Repeat with the remaining mixture.

CHICKEN
Pancakes

Prep Time: 6 mins
Total Time: 21 mins

Servings per Recipe: 4

Calories	321 kcal
Fat	17.8 g
Carbohydrates	9.6g
Protein	29.1 g
Cholesterol	116 mg
Sodium	441 mg

Ingredients

1 lb. skinless, boneless chicken breast
meat - finely chopped
1/2 medium onion, finely chopped
3 tbsp mayonnaise
1 egg, lightly beaten
1/3 C. all-purpose flour

salt and pepper to taste
2 tbsp vegetable oil

Directions

1. In a large bowl, add the chicken, onion, mayonnaise, egg, flour, salt and pepper and mix till well combined.
2. In a skillet, heat the oil on medium heat.
3. Add about 1/4 C. of the chicken mixture into the skillet and cook till browned from both sides.
4. Repeat with the remaining mixture.
5. Serve hot.

Creamy Banana Filled Beer Crepes

🥣 Prep Time: 1 hr
🕐 Total Time: 1 hr 30 mins

Servings per Recipe: 8
Calories	516 kcal
Fat	27 g
Carbohydrates	61.3g
Protein	7.7 g
Cholesterol	135 mg
Sodium	231 mg

Ingredients

1 C. all-purpose flour
1 C. stale beer, room temperature
4 eggs, room temperature
2 tbsps vegetable oil
1/4 tsp ground nutmeg
1/4 tsp salt
4 bananas, sliced 1/4-inch thick
1 lemon, juiced
1 (8 ounce) package cream cheese
1/4 C. brown sugar

1 C. whipped topping
1 C. white sugar
1/2 C. boiling water
3 tbsps cornstarch
1/2 C. water
3 tbsps butter
8 tsps vegetable oil, divided

Directions

1. In a large bowl, add the flour, nutmeg, salt, eggs, beer and 2 tbsps of oil and beat till smooth.
2. In a second bowl, add the sliced banana and lemon juice and toss to coat well.
3. In a third bowl, add the brown sugar and cream cheese and beat till fluffy and light.
4. Gently, fold in the whipped topping.
5. In a pan, add the white sugar on medium heat and cook, stirring continuously for about 2-4 minutes till melted.
6. Remove the pan from heat and immediately, stir in boiling water.
7. Return the pan on heat and cook, stirring till a clear syrup forms.
8. In a small bowl, mix together the water and cornstarch.
9. Slowly, add the cornstarch mixture in the pa, beating continuously and reduce the heat to low.
10. Simmer, stirring continuously for about 5-7 minutes.
11. Add the butter and beat till a caramel sauce forms.

12. Grease a crepe pan with 1 tsp of oil and heat on medium heat.
13. Place about 1/4 C. of the mixture and tilt the pan to spread it evenly.
14. Cook everything on both sides till golden brown.
15. Repeat with the remaining mixture.
16. Place about 2 tbsps of the caramel sauce in the center of each crepe, followed by cream cheese mixture and banana slices and roll around the filling.
17. Serve with a drizzling of the remaining caramel sauce.

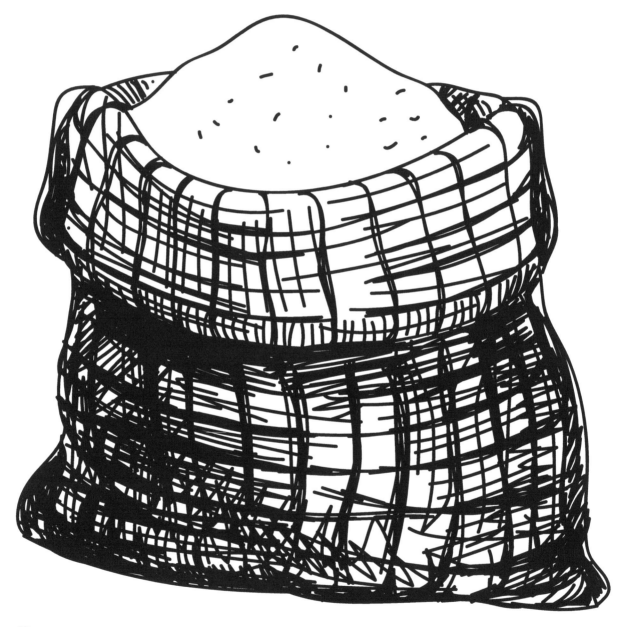

Apple Filled Crepes

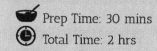 Prep Time: 30 mins

Total Time: 2 hrs

Servings per Recipe: 8

Calories	361 kcal
Fat	14.8 g
Carbohydrates	50.4g
Protein	7.9 g
Cholesterol	75 mg
Sodium	127 mg

Ingredients

3 eggs
1/4 tsp salt
2 C. all-purpose flour
2 C. milk
1/4 C. vegetable oil
1/2 tsp ground cinnamon
4 Granny Smith apples, peeled and diced
1/2 C. white sugar

2 tsps cinnamon
2 tbsps water
2 tbsps cornstarch
1 tbsp water
1 1/2 tbsps milk
8 tsps vegetable oil, divided

Directions

1. In a bowl, add the eggs and salt and beat well.
2. Slowly, add the flour, beating continuously, followed by 2 C. of milk till well combined.
3. Add 1/4 C. of the oil and 1/2 tsp of the cinnamon and beat till smooth and refrigerate, covered for at least 1 hour.
4. In another bowl, mix together the apples, 2 tbsps of the water, sugar and the remaining cinnamon.
5. In a small bowl, mix together the cornstarch and remaining water and transfer the mixture into the bowl of the apples mixture.
6. In a pan, add the apples mixture on medium heat and cook, stirring occasionally for about 8-10 minutes.
7. Grease a crepe pan with 1 tsp of oil and heat on medium heat.
8. Place about 1/3 C. of the mixture and tilt the pan to spread it evenly.
9. Cook for about 30 seconds and carefully, flip it. Cook till golden brown.
10. Repeat with the remaining mixture.
11. Divide the apple mixture in the center of the crepes evenly and roll around the filling.
12. Serve immediately.

NUTMEG
Coconut Filled Crepes

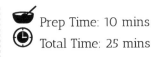

Prep Time: 10 mins
Total Time: 25 mins

Servings per Recipe: 8

Calories	203 kcal
Fat	8 g
Carbohydrates	26.5g
Protein	6.2 g
Cholesterol	59 mg
Sodium	252 mg

Ingredients

1 1/2 C. all-purpose flour
1 tbsp white sugar
1/2 tsp baking powder
1/2 tsp salt
2 C. milk
2 tbsps butter, melted
2 eggs

1/2 tsp vanilla extract
2 tsps vegetable oil
1/2 C. flaked coconut
1 tbsp white sugar
1/4 tsp ground cardamom

Directions

1. In a large bowl, sift together 1 tbsp of the sugar, flour, baking powder and salt.
2. Add butter, milk, eggs and vanilla and beat till smooth.
3. Lightly, grease a skillet with vegetable oil and heat on medium-high heat.
4. Place about 1/4 C. of the mixture and tilt the pan to spread it evenly.
5. Cook for about 2 minutes and carefully, flip it.
6. Cook for about 2 minutes.
7. Repeat with the remaining mixture.
8. In a bowl, mix together the remaining ingredients.
9. Divide the coconut mixture in the center of the crepes evenly and roll around the filling and serve.

Anise
& Orange Crepes

Prep Time: 10 mins
Total Time: 8 hrs 20 mins

Servings per Recipe: 6

Calories	213 kcal
Fat	8.2 g
Carbohydrates	25.5g
Protein	7.9 g
Cholesterol	137 mg
Sodium	91 mg

Ingredients

4 large eggs
1 C. milk
3/4 C. orange juice
1 tbsp anise extract
1 C. all-purpose flour

2 tbsps butter, divided
Sugar, for dusting

Directions

1. In a large bowl, add all the ingredients except butter and sugar and beat till smooth.
2. Lightly, grease a skillet with butter and heat on medium-high heat.
3. Place about 1/4 C. of the mixture and tilt the pan to spread it evenly.
4. Cook for about 2 minutes per side.
5. Repeat with the remaining mixture.
6. Serve with a sprinkling of a sugar.

CHOCO HAZELNUT
Banana Filled Crepes

 Prep Time: 20 mins

Total Time: 30 mins

Servings per Recipe: 4

Calories	236 kcal
Fat	8.6 g
Carbohydrates	35.1g
Protein	4.1 g
Cholesterol	70 mg
Sodium	58 mg

Ingredients

Crepe Batter:
1/2 C. whole or milk
1 1/2 tbsps melted butter
1 egg yolk
1 tsp vanilla
2 tsps hazelnut liqueur
1 tbsp cocoa
2 tbsps confectioners' sugar
1/3 C. white flour

Chocolate Sauce:
1/2 tbsp butter
1 tbsp whole or milk
2 tsps hazelnut liqueur
1 tbsp cocoa
2 tbsps confectioners' sugar
2 ripe bananas, sliced

Directions

1. In a large bowl, add the egg yolk, 1 1/2 tbsps of melted butter, 1/2 C. of milk, 2 tsps of hazelnut liqueur and vanilla and mix well.
2. Add the cocoa powder and beat till well combined.
3. Add the confectioner's sugar and beat till well combined.
4. Slowly, add the flour, beating continuously till well combined and keep aside.
5. In a pan, melt the remaining butter on low heat and stir in the remaining ingredients except banana slices.Keep the pan on very low heat to keep it warm.
6. Lightly, grease a crepe pan and heat on medium heat.
7. Place about 1/4 C. of the mixture and tilt the pan to spread it evenly.
8. Cook for about 2 minutes and carefully, flip it.
9. Cook for about 1 minute. Repeat with the remaining mixture.
10. In serving plates, arrange the crepes.
11. Place about 1/4 of the banana slices over each crepe and top with sauce evenly.
12. Roll the crepes around the filling and serve with a sprinkling of a confectioner's sugar.

Spiced
Flax Seeds Crepes

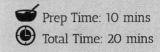 Prep Time: 10 mins

Total Time: 20 mins

Servings per Recipe: 4

Calories	331 kcal
Fat	22.3 g
Carbohydrates	23.4g
Protein	10.5 g
Cholesterol	140 mg
Sodium	232 mg

Ingredients

3 eggs

1 C. soy milk

1/4 C. olive oil

1/2 C. all-purpose flour

1/4 C. whole wheat flour

2 tbsps flax seeds

1/4 tsp salt

1/4 tsp ground cinnamon

1/8 tsp ground nutmeg

1 tsp vegetable oil

Directions

1. In a large bowl, add the soy milk, olive oil and eggs and beat till well combined.
2. In another bowl, add the remaining ingredients except vegetable oil and beat till smooth.
3. Add the flour mixture into egg mixture and beat till well combined.
4. Lightly, grease a skillet and heat on medium heat.
5. Place about 1/4 of the mixture and tilt the pan to spread it evenly.
6. Cook for about 3-4 minutes and carefully, flip it.
7. Cook for about 1-2 minutes.
8. Repeat with the remaining mixture.

CURRIED CHICKEN
& Olives Filled Crepes

Prep Time: 30 mins
Total Time: 45 mins

Servings per Recipe: 7

Calories	430 kcal
Fat	21.2 g
Carbohydrates	32g
Protein	27.1 g
Cholesterol	155 mg
Sodium	1185 mg

Ingredients

CREPES
1 1/2 C. all-purpose flour
2 1/2 C. milk
3 eggs, beaten
2 tbsps vegetable oil
1/2 tsp salt
FILLING
1/4 C. butter
1 1/4 C. diced celery
1 C. diced onion
2 tbsps all-purpose flour
1 tsp salt

3/4 tsp curry powder
1 C. milk
2 cubes chicken bouillon
1/2 C. warm water
3/4 C. sliced black olives
2 1/2 C. cooked, diced chicken breast meat
1/4 C. freshly grated Parmesan cheese

Directions

1. Set your oven to 400 degrees F before doing anything else.
2. For the crepes, in a large bowl, add the all the ingredients and beat till smooth.
3. Lightly, grease a skillet and heat on medium heat.
4. Place the desired amount of the mixture and tilt the pan to spread it evenly.
5. Cook till golden brown from one side.
6. Repeat with the remaining mixture.
7. For the filling, in a large skillet, melt the butter on medium heat and sauté the onion and celery till tender.
8. Stir in the flour, curry powder and salt till well combined.
9. In a bowl, mix together the warm water and bouillon.
10. Add the bouillon mixture and milk in the skillet, stirring continuously till the mixture becomes thick.

11. Stir in chicken and olives.

12. Divide the filling mixture in the center of the crepes evenly and roll around the filling.

13. Arrange the crepe rolls, seam side down into a 13x9-inch baking dish in a single layer.

14. Place the cheese over rolls evenly and cook in the oven for about 12 minutes.

MACARONI
and Eggs

Prep Time: 10 mins
Total Time: 25 mins

Servings per Recipe: 4
Calories	243 kcal
Fat	8.5 g
Carbohydrates	29.9 g
Protein	11.5 g
Cholesterol	194 mg
Sodium	93 mg

Ingredients

1 1/2 cups elbow macaroni
1 tbsp butter
1/4 tsp paprika (optional)

salt and ground black pepper to taste
4 large eggs, lightly beaten

Directions

1. Boil macaroni in salt and water for 9 mins until al dente.
2. Get a frying pan and melt some butter in it. Then add in your pasta to the melted butter along with some: pepper, paprika, and salt.
3. Add eggs to the pasta and do not stir anything for 2 mins. Then for 6 mins continue cooking the eggs but now you can stir. Turn off the heat.
4. Place a lid on the pan and let the eggs continue to cook without heat.

Florentine
Style

🍳 Prep Time: 10 mins
🕐 Total Time: 20 mins

Servings per Recipe: 3
Calories	279 kcal
Fat	22.9 g
Carbohydrates	4.1g
Protein	15.7 g
Cholesterol	408 mg
Sodium	276 mg

Ingredients

2 tbsps butter
1/2 cup mushrooms, sliced
2 cloves garlic, minced
1/2 (10 oz.) package fresh spinach

6 large eggs, slightly beaten
salt and ground black pepper to taste
3 tbsps cream cheese, cut into small pieces

Directions

1. Fry your garlic and mushrooms in melted butter in a frying pan for 2 mins. Then mix in your spinach and cook this for another 4 mins.
2. Finally add some pepper and salt and your eggs to the mix and let the eggs set completely. Once the eggs have set you want to flip them.
3. Add a bit of cream cheese to the eggs and let it cook for about 4 mins.

SCRAMBLED EGGS
Done Right

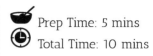 Prep Time: 5 mins
Total Time: 10 mins

Servings per Recipe: 1
Calories	420 kcal
Fat	33.1 g
Carbohydrates	9.7g
Protein	23.1 g
Cholesterol	575 mg
Sodium	755 mg

Ingredients

3 large eggs
1 pinch red pepper flakes
9 cherry tomatoes, halved
2 tbsps crumbled feta cheese
1 tbsp very thinly sliced fresh basil
leaves

olive oil
1 pinch sea salt

Directions

1. Get a bowl and evenly mix the following: basil, eggs, feta, red pepper flakes, and tomatoes.
2. Fry in hot olive oil for a few secs without any stirring so the eggs set. Then begin to scramble them for 1 min.
3. Ideally you want your eggs to be only lightly set. Remove them from the heat. Season with salt.
4. Enjoy.

Chipotle
Bacon and Eggs

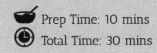 Prep Time: 10 mins

Total Time: 30 mins

Servings per Recipe: 4

Calories	381 kcal
Fat	29.6 g
Carbohydrates	12.2g
Protein	20.5 g
Cholesterol	310 mg
Sodium	553 mg

Ingredients

4 slices turkey bacon, chopped
6 eggs
2 tbsps sour cream
1 tbsp oil, or as needed
1 tbsp chipotle-flavored hot sauce (such as Tabasco(R) Chipotle Pepper Sauce)

3 vine-ripened tomatoes, chopped
1 avocado - peeled, pitted, and chopped
1 (6 oz.) package fresh spinach
1/2 cup shredded Cheddar cheese
salt and ground black pepper to taste

Directions

1. Get a bowl, evenly mix: sour cream and eggs.
2. Fry your bacon for 11 mins. Then remove oil excess with some paper towels.
3. Now you want to cook your eggs in oil in a frying pan for 7 minutes with your hot sauce.
4. Add in your spinach, avocadoes and tomatoes and cook for 1 more min.
5. Finally top everything with cheddar and a bit more pepper and salt. Let the cheese melt with another .5 to 1 min of cooking time.

BREAKFAST EGGS
from India

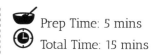

Prep Time: 5 mins
Total Time: 15 mins

Servings per Recipe: 2
Calories	367 kcal
Fat	32.9 g
Carbohydrates	12.4g
Protein	8.4 g
Cholesterol	186 mg
Sodium	157 mg

Ingredients

1/4 cup vegetable oil
1 tsp garam masala
1 tsp ground turmeric
1 tsp ground coriander
salt to taste
1/2 cup finely chopped onion

3 green chili peppers, sliced
2 large eggs

Directions

1. Get a bowl and add your eggs to it. Then whisk them.
2. In a frying pan, cook the following in hot oil for 6 mins: salt, green chili peppers, garam masala, onions, coriander, and turmeric.
3. After 6 mins pour in your eggs to the seasoned onions and chilies and scramble for 5 mins.

Fried Eggs and Shrimp

🥄 Prep Time: 10 mins

🕐 Total Time: 25 mins

Servings per Recipe: 3

Calories	236 kcal
Fat	14.9 g
Carbohydrates	8.8g
Protein	16.8 g
Cholesterol	404 mg
Sodium	1237 mg

Ingredients

1 tbsp vegetable oil, or as needed
1 onion, chopped
6 eggs, beaten
1 tsp salt

10 cooked large shrimp
1/4 cup cocktail sauce

Directions

1. Fry onions in hot oil for 11 mins. Then mix in the eggs and salt. Continue frying for 6 mins.

2. Add in your shrimp and cocktail sauce and continue to cook for 5 more mins.

3. Enjoy.

MAGGIE'S
Favorite Eggs

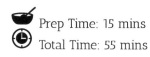

Prep Time: 15 mins
Total Time: 55 mins

Servings per Recipe: 8
Calories   492 kcal
Fat   38.2 g
Carbohydrates   12.8g
Protein   27 g
Cholesterol   343 mg
Sodium   1683 mg

Ingredients

1 (1 lb) bulk beef sausage
12 eggs, beaten
1/3 cup sour cream
1 (7 oz.) can chopped green chilies
1 (24 oz.) jar salsa
1 cup shredded Cheddar cheese

1 cup shredded Monterey Jack cheese
1/2 cup pickled jalapeno pepper slices, or to taste
2 avocados, sliced

Directions

1. Coat a baking dish with oil or nonstick spray and set your oven to 350 degrees before doing anything else.
2. Get a bowl and whisk all your eggs together in it. Enter the eggs into the greased dish. And bake it in the oven for 15 mins.
3. For 8 mins fry your sausage in hot oil and then crumble.
4. After eggs have baked for 15 mins remove them from the oven layer your sausage, jalapeno, salsa, green chilies, Monterey, and cheddar over the eggs.
5. Put everything back in the oven for 23 mins.
6. Enjoy. With a topping of avocado.

Egg Salad

Prep Time: 10 mins
Total Time: 10 mins

Servings per Recipe: 8

Calories	83 kcal
Fat	5.3 g
Carbohydrates	1.3g
Protein	6.8 g
Cholesterol	212 mg
Sodium	141 mg

Ingredients

8 hard-cooked eggs, chopped
1/4 cup plain fat-free yogurt
1 tbsp parsley flakes
1/4 tsp onion powder

1/4 tsp paprika
1/4 tsp salt

Directions

1. To make this salad get a bowl: and combine all the ingredients until completely smooth and even.
2. Enjoy with toasted bread.

EASY
Spicy Eggs

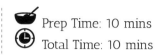

Prep Time: 10 mins
Total Time: 10 mins

Servings per Recipe: 4

Calories	46 kcal
Fat	3.4 g
Carbohydrates	0.4g
Protein	3.3 g
Cholesterol	108 mg
Sodium	33 mg

Ingredients

2 hard-cooked eggs, cut in half
lengthwise
1 tbsp cream-style horseradish sauce

Directions

1. Take your eggs and take out the yolks. Put the yolks aside in a bowl.
2. Add horseradish to the yolks and mix everything evenly.
3. Simply fill each egg white with the yolk mix and chill before serving them.

The Maine
Frittata

🥄 Prep Time: 10 mins
🕐 Total Time: 25 mins

Servings per Recipe: 2
Calories   603.0 kcal
Cholesterol   531.5mg
Sodium   342.7mg
Carbohydrates   39.0g
Protein   26.1g

Ingredients

5 eggs
1/3 C. cream
1/2 tsp shredded lemon rind
5 drops hot sauce
salt and pepper, to taste
3 tbsps shredded sharp cheddar cheese

1 large potato, diced
1 small onion, chopped
1 tbsp oil
1/4 C. chopped bell pepper
1 C. crabmeat, fresh frozen, canned

Directions

1. Get a bowl, combine: pepper, eggs, salt, tabasco, and lemon rind.
2. Place your potato and onions in a separate bowl and put them in the microwave for 4 mins with the highest power setting.
3. Now begin to stir fry the onions and potatoes in oil until they are done then add in the capsicum and continue to cook the mix for 2 more mins.
4. Pour in the egg mix then break the crabmeat over everything.
5. Cook the mix for 6 mins then place it under the broiler for 2 to 3 more mins.
6. Enjoy.

EASY
Bacon Frittata

Prep Time: 20 mins
Total Time: 40 mins

Servings per Recipe: 4
Calories   297.4 kcal
Cholesterol   401.7mg
Sodium   317.8mg
Carbohydrates   5.5g
Protein   16.0g

Ingredients

1 red pepper, chopped
6 green onions, chopped
8 slices turkey bacon, sliced into small
pieces
8 eggs
1/2 C. half-and-half

1 tbsp butter
salt and pepper

Directions

1. Set your oven to 350 degrees before doing anything else.
2. Now begin to fry your bacon in butter until it is fully done. Then add in the veggies and let them cook until they are soft.
3. At the same time get a bowl, whisk: pepper, salt, half and half, and the eggs.
4. Beat the mix until it is smooth then pour it into the pan once the veggies are soft.
5. Let the frittata cook for about 6 mins until the bottom is set then place everything into the oven for 12 mins.
6. Enjoy.

Peppers and Mozzarella Frittata

Prep Time: 15 mins
Total Time: 35 mins

Servings per Recipe: 6
Calories   401.5 kcal
Cholesterol   216.6mg
Sodium   448.7mg
Carbohydrates   30.1g
Protein   24.3g

Ingredients

1 onion, chopped
1 green bell pepper, chopped
1 red sweet bell pepper, chopped
2 tbsps margarine
1 (7 oz.) box spaghetti, cooked
1 (8 oz.) package shredded mozzarella cheese
5 eggs

1 C. milk
1/3 C. shredded parmesan cheese
1 tbsp dried basil
1 tsp oregano
1 tsp seasoning salt
1/2 tsp white pepper

Directions

1. Set your oven to 375 degrees before doing anything else.
2. Stir fry your peppers and onions in margarine for 7 mins.
3. Get a bowl and toss your spaghetti and onion-pepper mix. Then add in the mozzarella and stir everything.
4. Pour the mix into a casserole dish that has been coated with butter then place a covering of foil over everything.
5. Let the mix cook for 17 mins then remove the foil and cook everything for 4 more mins.
6. Enjoy.

GOUDA
and Artichoke Frittata

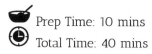

Prep Time: 10 mins
Total Time: 40 mins

Servings per Recipe: 1
Calories	249.0 kcal
Cholesterol	272.5mg
Sodium	457.6mg
Carbohydrates	8.3g
Protein	16.8g

Ingredients

2 tbsps butter
1/2 C. chopped shallot
2 C. artichoke hearts, diced
4 C. baby spinach leaves
10 eggs, beaten
1/4 tsp salt

1/4 tsp cayenne pepper
1/2 lb gouda cheese, shredded

Directions

1. Set your oven to 400 degrees before doing anything else.
2. Begin to stir fry your shallots in butter for 60 secs then add in the artichokes and cook them for 60 secs before adding and the spinach and cooking the leaves until they are soft.
3. Now add in your eggs evenly, covering the entire surface of the pan, and let everything cook over a low to medium level of heat for 12 mins.
4. Top everything with the cheese and place the pan in the oven for 17 mins.
5. Enjoy.

The Greek Style
Frittata

🥄 Prep Time: 45 mins
🕐 Total Time: 1 hr 20 mins

Servings per Recipe: 6
Calories   288.5 kcal
Cholesterol   301.7mg
Sodium   656.5mg
Carbohydrates   5.6g
Protein   15.2g

Ingredients

8 pitted kalamata olives, chopped
1 medium zucchini, cut into 1/2-inch cubes
1 sweet red pepper, chopped
1/2 C. onion, chopped
1/4 C. olive oil
9 large eggs, lightly beaten
1 (4 oz.) packages crumbled feta cheese

1/3 C. fresh basil, thinly sliced
1/2 tsp salt
1/2 tsp pepper
1/3 C. freshly shredded parmesan cheese

Directions

1. Stir fry your onions, red pepper, zucchini cubes, and olives in olive oil until everything is soft.
2. Now get a bowl, combine: eggs, feta, basil, pepper, and salt.
3. Whisk the mix until it is smooth then add it to the veggie mix.
4. Place a lid on the pan and let the mix cook for 10 mins then top it with the parmesan and place the pan under the broiler for 4 mins with the broiler door slightly ajar.
5. Enjoy.

THE PORTUGUESE
Frittata

Prep Time: 5 mins
Total Time: 25 mins

Servings per Recipe: 1
Calories	380.2 kcal
Cholesterol	438.2mg
Sodium	791.8mg
Carbohydrates	14.7g
Protein	20.4g

Ingredients

3 tbsps extra virgin olive oil
1/4 lb chorizo sausage, casing removed and chopped
2 large boiling potatoes, cut in half and thinly slice
1 small onion, thinly sliced
4 garlic cloves, chopped
12 eggs

1/3 C. half-and-half
1 tsp salt
black pepper
1/4 lb manchego cheese, shredded
1/2 C. flat leaf parsley, chopped

Directions

1. Set your oven to 400 degrees before doing anything else.
2. Begin to stir fry your chorizo in extra virgin olive oil for 4 mins then add in the onions and potatoes.
3. Cook the mix for 6 more mins then add the garlic and cook the garlic for 2 mins.
4. Get a bowl, whisk: pepper, salt, half and half, and the eggs.
5. Whisk the mix until it is smooth.
6. Add the eggs to the chorizo mix and let the bottom set. Lift the edges of the frittata to cook more eggs then top everything with cheese once the bottom of the frittata is fully set.
7. Place the pan in the oven for 14 mins.
8. Top it with some parsley after it has cooled for 7 mins.
9. Enjoy.

The Athenian Frittata

Prep Time: 15 mins
Total Time: 1 hr 5 mins

Servings per Recipe: 8
Calories   411.0 kcal
Cholesterol   306.1mg
Sodium   553.2mg
Carbohydrates   28.5g
Protein   23.2g

Ingredients

5 potatoes, sliced
1/4 C. olive oil
1 C. onion, chopped
1/4 C. green pepper, chopped
3 garlic cloves, minced
4 C. frozen chopped broccoli
12 eggs, beaten
3/4 C. parmesan cheese, shredded

1/2 C. water
1 tsp dried basil leaves
1/2 tsp salt
1/2 tsp black pepper
1 1/2 C. Monterey jack cheese, shredded (6 oz)

Directions

1. Set your oven to 350 degrees before doing anything else.
2. Stir fry your potatoes in oil for 12 mins then combine in the garlic, onion, and green pepper.
3. Stir the fry the mix until everything is soft then combine in the broccoli, place a lid on the pot, and let everything cook for 7 mins.
4. Layer your veggies into a casserole dish.
5. Get a bowl, combine: pepper, eggs, salt, parmesan, basil, and water. Whisk the mix until it is smooth then pour the eggs into the casserole dish evenly.
6. Top everything with the Monterey and cook the frittata in the oven for 27 mins.
7. Enjoy.

THE GRANNY SMITH
Frittata

Prep Time: 25 mins
Total Time: 32 mins

Servings per Recipe: 4
Calories   133.3 kcal
Cholesterol   211.5mg
Sodium   129.8mg
Carbohydrates   11.4g
Protein   10.4g

Ingredients

4 large eggs
4 large egg whites
1 large apple, granny smith, peeled and
julienned
1 medium leek, rinsed well and thinly
sliced
1 tbsp fresh sage, chopped
sage leaf

cooking spray
salt and pepper

Directions

1. Get a bowl, combine your egg whites and eggs. Whisk the mix together until everything is smooth.
2. Begin to stir fry your leeks in nonstick spray for 3 mins then stir in the apples and cook everything for 4 more mins.
3. Now add some pepper, salt, and the sage. Stir the spice into the apples and leeks.
4. Evenly distribute the leeks and apples in the pan then add in your eggs evenly as well.
5. Make sure the bottom surface of the pan is completely covered. Then set the heat to low and place a lid on the pan.
6. Let the frittata cook for 5 mins until it is fully done.
7. Top it with more sage.
8. Enjoy.

Zucchini and Cheddar Frittata

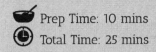 Prep Time: 10 mins
Total Time: 25 mins

Servings per Recipe: 4
Calories	282.1 kcal
Cholesterol	437.8mg
Sodium	234.0mg
Carbohydrates	12.1g
Protein	18.0g

Ingredients

8 eggs, lightly beaten
1 tbsp fresh basil or 1 tsp dried basil, crushed
1 tbsp olive oil
1 C. frozen whole kernel corn
1/2 C. thinly sliced zucchini
3 green onions, thinly sliced
3/4 C. chopped roma tomato

1/2 C. shredded cheddar cheese

Directions

1. Get a bowl, combine: basil and eggs.
2. Begin to stir fry your zucchini, corn, and green onions in olive oil for 5 mins then combine in the tomatoes and cook everything for 6 more mins.
3. Top the veggies with the eggs and let the bottom portion of the eggs set while lifting the edges to get more of the eggs cooked.
4. Once the bottom is fully set, top the frittata with cheese and place everything in the broiler for 3 mins.
5. Enjoy.

THE SEATTLE
Frittata

Prep Time: 5 mins
Total Time: 25 mins

Servings per Recipe: 6
Calories	247.6 kcal
Cholesterol	236.4mg
Sodium	325.3mg
Carbohydrates	4.3g
Protein	14.5g

Ingredients

8 frozen artichoke hearts, drained
2 garlic cloves, minced
1 medium onion, cut in crescents
3 tbsps olive oil
6 eggs
1/2 C. milk
1/2 tsp dried oregano
1/8 tsp pepper

1 C. mozzarella cheese, shredded
1/2 C. shredded parmesan cheese
fresh basil leaf

Directions

1. Cook the artichoke in a pan with nonstick spray until they are soft. Then divide each piece of artichoke and place them to the side.
2. Now get your oven's broiler hot before doing anything else.
3. Begin to stir fry your garlic and onions in 2 tbsp of olive oil until it is brown.
4. Get a bowl, combine: half of the parmesan, eggs, mozzarella, milk, pepper, and oregano. Whisk the mix until it is smooth then add in the onion mix.
5. Add the rest of the olive oil to the frying pan and evenly layer your pieces of artichoke into the pan.
6. Now add your eggs and set the heat to low.
7. Place a lid on the pan and let the frittata cook for 12 mins then top it with the rest of the parmesan and place everything under the broiler for 3 mins.
8. Top the frittata with some basil.
9. Enjoy.

Tasty
Swiss Chard Frittata

🥣 Prep Time: 10 mins
🕐 Total Time: 1 hr 10 mins

Servings per Recipe: 6
Calories	734.7 kcal
Cholesterol	598.1mg
Sodium	1821.5mg
Carbohydrates	12.0g
Protein	45.3g

Ingredients

1 1/2 lbs bulk Italian sausage
8 oz. fresh mushrooms, sliced
2 tbsps butter
1 garlic clove, minced
3 large Swiss chard leaves, rolled and sliced thin
1 C. mild cheddar cheese, shredded
14 large eggs

1 3/4 C. milk
2 tbsps Dijon mustard
sour cream
chopped green onions

Directions

1. Set your oven to 350 degrees before doing anything else.
2. Fry your sausage in a frying pan then remove the excess oils.
3. Place the sausages evenly into a casserole dish then begin to stir-fry your garlic and mushrooms in butter until everything is absorbed.
4. Top the sausage with the mushroom mix.
5. Now lay your Swiss chard over the mushrooms and then layer the cheese.
6. Get a bowl, combine: Dijon, milk, and eggs.
7. Whisk the mix until it is smooth then top the Swiss chards with the egg mix.
8. Cook the frittata in the oven for 60 mins then cover the dish with foil and let everything sit for 17 more mins.
9. Garnish the frittata with sour cream and green onions.
10. Enjoy.

THE SIMPLE
Chives Frittata

Prep Time: 10 mins
Total Time: 40 mins

Servings per Recipe: 8
Calories	128.9 kcal
Cholesterol	224.0mg
Sodium	146.0mg
Carbohydrates	1.1g
Protein	9.8g

Ingredients

8 eggs
2 tbsps water
1 C. shredded colby-monterey jack
cheese, divided
1/2 C. fresh chives, chopped

1/2 C. minced red bell pepper
1/2 tsp fresh ground black pepper

Directions

1. Set your oven to 350 degrees before doing anything else.
2. Get a bowl and beat your eggs in it then add in: 1/2 C. of cheese, herbs, black pepper, and bell pepper.
3. Combine the mix until it is smooth then coat a pie dish with nonstick spray.
4. Add the wet mix to the pan and evenly then top it with the rest of the cheese.
5. Cook the frittata in the oven for 35 mins then top it with some more herbs.
6. Enjoy.

The Pepper
Jack Pepper Frittata

Prep Time: 10 mins
Total Time: 40 mins

Servings per Recipe: 8
Calories   128.9 kcal
Cholesterol   224.0mg
Sodium   146.0mg
Carbohydrates   1.1g
Protein   9.8g

Ingredients

8 eggs
2 tbsps water
1 C. shredded pepper jack cheese, divided
1/2 C. fresh tarragon

1/2 C. minced red bell pepper
1/2 tsp fresh ground black pepper

Directions

1. Set your oven to 350 degrees before doing anything else.
2. Get a bowl, combine: water and eggs.
3. Stir the mix until it is smooth then add in half a C. of cheese, tarragon, black pepper, and bell peppers.
4. Stir the mix until it is smooth then top it with the rest of the cheese.
5. Enter everything into a pie dish then cook the frittata in the oven for 35 mins.
6. Enjoy.

THE GARDEN
Frittata

Prep Time: 5 mins
Total Time: 15 mins

Servings per Recipe: 4
Calories	211.5 kcal
Cholesterol	339.7mg
Sodium	370.3mg
Carbohydrates	4.7g
Protein	14.4g

Ingredients

4 small yellow squash
1 tbsp butter
6 eggs
1/2 C. cheddar cheese, shredded
1 tsp italian seasoning

1/4 tsp salt
1/2 tsp pepper

Directions

1. Cut your squash into thin slices. Then fry them in butter until crispy.
2. Get a bowl, combine: pepper, eggs, salt, Italian seasoning, and shredded cheese.
3. Add the egg mix to the squash in the pan and let the mix cook for 10 mins with a low level of heat and a lid on the pot.
4. Now place the frittata under the broiler for 3 mins to cook the top.
5. Enjoy.

Fontina and Sun-Dried Frittata

Prep Time: 10 mins
Total Time: 20 mins

Servings per Recipe: 4

Calories	529.8 kcal
Cholesterol	259.1mg
Sodium	1450.8mg
Carbohydrates	47.4g
Protein	26.8g

Ingredients

8 oz. spaghetti
1/2 C. sun-dried tomato packed in oil, drained and chopped
4 large eggs
1 1/2 tsps salt
1/2 tsp ground black pepper
3/4 C. parmesan cheese, shredded
3/4 C. Fontina cheese, shredded
1 tbsp butter
1 tbsp extra virgin olive oil

Directions

1. Boil your spaghetti in water and salt for 9 mins then remove the liquids and combine the pasta with the sun dried tomatoes.
2. Get a bowl and combine fontina, eggs, parmesan, pepper, and salt.
3. Stir the mix until it is smooth then stir in the eggs.
4. Place the mix into a large frying pan with hot butter and cook the mix for 4 mins with a medium level of heat.
5. Now put everything under the broiler for 6 mins.
6. Enjoy.

Printed in Great Britain
by Amazon